How to Build a Bottle Rocket

by Tristan Trubble

Published in USA by:

Tristan Trubble
P.O BOX #9
Boynton Beach
FL 33425

© Copyright 2017

ISBN-13: 978-1548285104
ISBN-10: 1548285102

Table of Contents

Chapter 1: What can a Bottle Rocket Be used for?

When it comes to bottle rockets there are a couple of different designs you can choose from that will work relatively well depending on how much attention to detail you employ during the process.

Bottle Rockets can be used for several various reasons. Families with younger children may find building a bottle rocket to be necessary for part of a science project. Educators in the science field like to use simple projects of this nature to provide examples for their students that can be used to describe or show how certain laws of physics function when applied correctly.

Being able to build a homemade bottle rocket can also be an enjoyable past time experience for the budding science prodigy. Once they have mastered the techniques of constructing their own functioning soda bottle rocket they will have a better understanding of how opposing forces work to propel a device over distance. They can then use this knowledge to modify or invent their own designs for more powerful projectiles using a variety of propellants.

For the most part, the homemade soda bottle rocket idea is used for entertainment purposes. They do not fly that high or far and due to the low cost of materials and crude construction practices they are viewed as expendable. They might work for a handful of launches before needing to be tossed out and replaced or they may last for several consecutive launches without deteriorating to the point of being unsafe to operate.

The majority of individuals that decide they would like to learn how to make a bottle rocket never think of how useful these devices might be for other purposes. If it is for a science project all they hope for is that it will stay together long enough to be successfully launched. After their demonstration has been witnessed and a grade received they may never touch the device again or if anything they will use it as a conversation hobby piece to show others how well it works.

For the rising science savant, the ability to manufacture a bottle rocket from common household items often leads to leaps in ingenuity. Some of these students take construction and performance issues very seriously and invent blue prints or alter features to try and modify the system to provide greater altitude or distance.

Very few people consider options outside the norm for making and using a bottle rocket system. We take several things for granted currently, our life expectancy among them, and very seldom, if at all, concern ourselves with what might happen should we wake up on the morrow with an apocalyptic landscape at our door step. Those of us that function as preparatory specialists bent on surviving might find homemade bottle rockets to a beneficial device to have available in the aftermath of a world ending event.

In the doomsday scenario, a homemade bottle rocket can be used as a signaling system to alert others within the survival compound of intruders. It can also be used similarly to alert others in a hunting party of a location where livestock are gathering, thereby allowing all hunters to congregate in a common location to hunt for food.
They might also be used as a deterrent to instill fear in an approaching unknown entity such as wandering survivors, or a large carnivorous animal.

The hand-crafted bottle rocket can also be used as a communication device to coordinate counterattacks. These devices can be constructed and placed at forward sentry positions. Should the headquarters of the survivalist compound come under attack the person at the sentry position can launch a bottle rocket in a specific direction to indicate where responding reinforcement troops should focus their efforts.

Depending on the layout of the complex and the defensive forward positions that are established a well-built bottle rocket might also be useful for sending and receiving messages. In an apocalyptic aftermath society of this nature these devices will replace the instant messaging systems of modern technology we enjoy today.

If we look back throughout the history of modern warfare we will come to realize that one of the most effectively used soldiers of any military was the 'runner.' This individual was a message courier and it was their sole responsibility to run between separated divisions to deliver messages that would allow them to continue coordinating their efforts. These soldiers were instrumental in ensuring a successful mission, even after the invention of field radios, since over the air communications could be intercepted, interpreted and used against the attacking force.

In a doomsday environment, the number of people who will survive will be severely limited. In most survivalist camps, there will not be enough manpower to provide resources for assigning someone as a message carrier to run between exterior facing defensive positions to coordinate a repelling counterattack. Short of using a bullhorn and alerting the insurgents to your plans for thwarting their advance you will need to develop ideas that will be useful to you and help ensure the safety and security of all those within the confines of the camp.

When used in conjunction with trip wires the homemade bottle rocket system can also be used separately as a signal flare that will alert those in the complex that something has crossed an outer boundary. Wildlife that has survived may gravitate towards a habitable complex that they can smell on the wind. With an early warning system in place the responding units can assemble on site and determine which actions need to be taken.

When used with trip wires and snaring pitfalls, a skyward bound bottle rocket will signal that a snare has been tripped and a potential food supply resource is available for the taking.

These alternate options for manufacturing homemade bottle rockets will come in handy should you and you survivalist citizens elect to employ them. If you and your cabal are living near another complex and have established an alliance with the same, then these devices will also serve the purpose of establishing an instant communication system between the two camps.

Chapter 2: The Materials for Manufacturing

Keep in mind that there are hundreds of different homemade bottle rocket designs that you can choose from. For this educational and instructional compilation, we will be focusing on a design that will be easy to produce without the use of power tools or explosives which may be hard to come by without proper permits and licenses. Electricity will more than likely be a distant memory for most people in a survivalist situation. If you elect to search for a different design, then pay special attention to this aspect, as plans that involve using power tools will be ineffective and cumbersome.

The list begins with the procurement of 2-liter pop bottles. You can use any style, shape or design so long as the entire bottle is intact and has not been dented, damaged or punctured as seen below.

You will also need an ample supply of poster board. This heavy-duty paper product will serve as the fins or guidance system for the rocket. It needs to be sturdy enough to support the weight of the bottle and the water used as part of the propellant.

These drafting triangles make a great template to use for cutting out the fins for the rocket. Lay one on the poster board, trace an outline and use the scissors to cut them out.

A sharp set of scissors comes next on the list. Dull scissors may work effectively enough to get the job done; however, a sharp set will make the process flow more smoothly and help prevent any adverse effects that might be cause by jagged or ripped cut lines.

Now you need a glue delivery system. Most of the instructions manuals you come across recommend a glue gun that has a low temperature setting. Since electricity in an apocalyptic aftermath probably won't be an available resource, we are going to substitute this for something that will be just as effective and easy to find. Grab several small bottles of instant adhesive. You will want to read the instructions on the product of choice to ensure it can be used with paper and plastic. Some adhesive compounds will eat holes through plastic; avoid using these solutions as they will destroy the project before it gets started.

Modeling clay is the next item on the shopping and supply list. This material is going to be used in the cone of the rocket to add weight to the top of the rocket and assist with ensuring the stability of the device while in flight. If you do not have the resources to transport this material you might be able to substitute it with homemade adobe or compacted mud once you are at your new location.

This is what you want the nose cone of your bottle rocket to look like. You can either fashion this out of the poster board or you can use Birthday Party hats of similar fashion for this purpose.

Duct Tape should be at or near the top of each survivalist's supply list. This material can be used for thousands upon thousands of homemade manufacturing processes. When used properly it can even be used as a tow rope for pulling a vehicle out of a sticky situation. Have it handy and use it to your advantage.

http://www.officemax.com/office-supplies has the type of poster board, tape and scissors you will need to construct your homemade bottle rocket.

Drinking straws in abundance also make the list of necessary materials. These are going to be attached to the rocket and used as connecting devices for the launch platform. Do not get the kind with a bendable end. The ridges present in the compressed section of the bend may interfere with proper launch procedures.

You will also need to look for an end cap solution. Rubber stoppers that are the same diameter as the neck opening of the soda bottle are the most commonly sought after items for this feature. As a simpler substitute, you might want to consider using cork instead of rubber. Another option might be soft wood that can be cut or fabricated to fit with a hole saw relatively easy. Regardless of what you decide to employ for your rocket this material needs to fit snugly and tightly within the bottle neck. If there are any gaps for water and air to escape, then the system will fail to achieve the desired effect.

A hand drill and drill bits should also be an item carried and available in the survivalist scenario. You will need to drill small holes in the stopper that will allow the air delivery system to be inserted.

A bicycle tire pump is the perfect solution for delivering pressurized air to the interior of the rocket. Make sure you have the complete pump including insertion needle. If you will be using these rockets with trip wires and traps, then grab an ample stockpile of these needles so they can be left in place on each device and used to trigger the system when a wire is tripped.

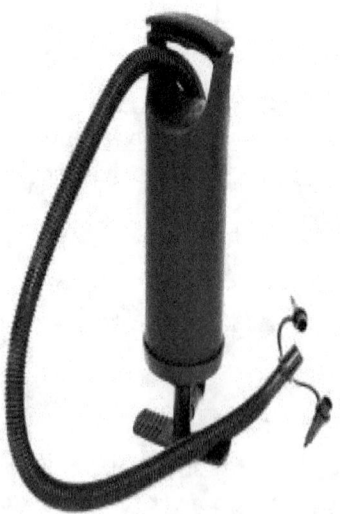

¼" diameter metal rods or a plethora of similar devices will serve as the launch platform for your homemade rocket systems. If you do not have these available then you can manufacture similar launch pad products from scratch. Small straight twigs and branches can be used as a substitute so long as you take time to whittle them into as straight and true a shape as possible. Be mindful of the fact that these items are going to be used to send the rocket in a given direction, if there are variances along the route the rocket may end up flying in a direction other than the desired path.

Colored markers paint and paint brushes will round out the list of supplies. The materials are generally used for cosmetic and aesthetic enhancement of the rocket itself. In a survivalist camp the rockets should be painted in a plethora of vibrant colors that are easy to recognize and differentiate. The color combinations used on the rockets will serve to facilitate communication. A red rocket might signal responding reinforcements to halt their advance on a defensive location, whereas a green rocket might signal the need for a rapid response to an affected area.

You can find a variety of bicycle and foot pumps at http://www.walmart.com/ip/Bell-Sports-Foot-Pumper-Multi-Sport-Pump/14003639 to use for injecting the air into the rocket.

These wooden skewers make an excellent rocket launching platform. Stick them in the ground at the appropriate dimensions and slide the straws attached to the rocket body over them.

Use your imagination. Experiment with the construction process and develop modifications according to your needs or desires. You will need ample water supply for your bottle rockets. Potable water may be in short supply so having a stagnant pond of standing water within the borders of the habitable zone will be an important concern to take into consideration. While the remainder of the rocket may be retrieved and possibly used again the water being employed will not be reusable and will need to be replaced. In the event a non-potable water supply is not immediately available set up catch buckets and collection systems for trapping rain water run-off. Save the good stuff for human consumption, it is a life sustaining commodity that should be guarded, not a resource you can take for granted any longer.

You can use this same list of materials and supplies to manufacture homemade bottle rockets of any size. 20 oz. and 1-liter pop bottles will work; however, they more than likely will not fly as high or far since they have less space for containing the pressurized air that serves as the fuel source.

Chapter 3: Seven Step Success System

Step #1: Rinse out the interior of the bottle of choice. This may not seem like an important step in the process; however, left over and dried on pop residue can cause the launched rocket to wobble in flight or veer from the desired flight path. Think about what you might be using these devices for. Do they need to fly straight and true to convey a specific message to a comrade on the other side of the camp?

Step #2: Wrap and glue one sheet of poster board around the pop bottle. Do not cover the bottom of the bottle or the opening at the neck. Glue the poster board in such a fashion as it creates what appears to be a cylinder shape, thereby masking the contours of the bottle shape. This will assist in ensuring stability during flight by providing a smooth exterior surface for air to flow over. If you leave the bottle bare, then the contours of the original design will influence the flight path.

Step #3: Cut another sheet of poster board to fabricate right angle fins. We have all seen what a 1950's depiction of a rocket ship looks like. They have three to four fins for stability and launch support. You need to recreate these objects for your own bottle rocket. Make sure they are all the same size and shape. If they vary in configuration the flight path of the projectile will remain undetermined. Make a ¼" bend along the longest side of the fin and use this to apply glue and attach each fin to the poster board cylinder sides of the bottle. Make sure they are equidistant from one another.

Step #4: Take a third piece of poster board and roll it into a cone shape. Cut the bottom edge of this cone in a straight line. Use a 3" ball of modeling clay and mash it into the top of the cone. Make sure not to use so much pressure you distort the shape of the cone, you just need the clay to stick to the top of the poster board. Glue this contraption to the bottom edge of the bottle which is now the top of the rocket.

Step #5: Using the duct tape, attach three straws to the exterior of the rocket near the fins. Make sure to allow them to hang below the base of the fins. These do not necessarily have to be of the same length or exact position as far as length of exposure is concerned. Drill a small hole in the rubber stopper that is as close to the diameter of the bike tire pump needle.

Step #6: This step involves filling the bottle with water. You will want to use your first finished rocket system as an experimental device to discover how much fluid is going to be sufficient to launch the device to the desired height and distance. Start out filling the bottle ¼ of the way full. If this does not meet or exceed your expectations, then adjust the amount to ½ full and repeat the launch. Continue this process until satisfied; however, do not exceed filling the bottle past ¾ capacity as there will be very little room for pressurized air and the weight of additional fluid may keep the rocket grounded rather than send it skyward. Seal with the rubber stopper.

Step #7: Assemble three of the metal rods to correspond with the straws on the side of the rocket and place them firmly in the ground at the launch location. Slide the straw supports over the metal rods. Insert the needle of the bike pump into the hole on the rubber stopper. Begin pumping the air from the bike pump.

When the pressure inside the rocket reaches maximum capacity, the stopper will erupt from the bottom of the rocket and send the projectile up into the air in the direction indicated by the launch platform.

These instructions provide the basic launch mechanism and platform for mass manufacturing of hand crafted bottle rocket devices. As stated previously you are free to make modifications as you see fit to develop and design a system with greater launch capabilities and performance expectations.

With a little ingenuity and knowledge this basic bottle rocket concept can be altered to include additional offensive or defensive measures. You may want to research and discover other flammable fluid solutions to substitute for water. When the rocket is launched the flammable liquid will spray out behind the projectile and can then be lit to ignite a wall of fire. Intruders are less likely to attempt to break through a fire wall than they are an open area being ogled by a static sentry post.

You may also want to modify the cone area of the comet by inserting a sharp pointy metallic object which will serve as a spear. If you have honed the rocket firing guidance system to provide pinpoint accuracy, then a spear attachment can cause immediate damage to an assailant when fired in their direction.

Self-preservation in a survivalist scenario will require using a vivid and intuitive imagination. Look at every item you have at your disposal in a different light. This includes manmade manufactured products as well as elements you can find in nature. A hardwood stick can be shaved into a spear shape and substituted for a metallic counterpart.

You might want to research parachute retrieval systems that can be used in conjunction with a bottle rocket of this nature. While retrieval of the system may not be high on the priority list for items of this nature, a parachute attachment will increase the hang time of the device while it is airborne and allow for longer periods of signal identification for those it is intended to alert.

Use the color combination schemes you create effectively. Assign specific meanings to each color. It might also be wise to develop a codified location identification system, where each forward position or trap location has a very specific and separate color associated with it. This will eliminate confusion when an immediate response is needed, regardless of how accurate or errant the device is. For instance, a bright blue color scheme might indicate that the lookout post in the NW quadrant of the compound is under attack, whereas a vibrant yellow might require a response to the SE sector of the same complex.

Just because you woke up the morning after the apocalypse and the rest of the world remained in eternal slumber, do not assume that you can defeat or overcome all obstacles you will face as you move forward. Your survival is going to rely on many things, the ability to think outside the box and make on the spot judgments and decisions will be at the top of this list. There will be no rules to govern your actions, so visualize, design, develop and experiment at will until you have achieved the level of success desired.

Chapter 4: Additional Ideas to Consider

So far, we have discussed a few ideas about using the bottle rocket for survivalist scenarios to prevent or thwart an advancing and aggressive adversary. We have hinted at making modifications to further enhance the performance capabilities of the system for many different uses.

In this section, we are going to discuss preparing the habitable bunker for an actual doomsday event. If you haven't just run out and dug a hole in the dirt to hide your family, friends, supplies and resources, you should have a well-designed blue print of the compound you will be living at after the catastrophe takes place.

As part of your bunker blue print you might find it helpful to install and implement tubing delivery systems throughout the complex. PVC pipe and fittings can be assembled and buried in between routes of expected communication, thereby linking every forward position with the command center as well as each other. In many cases a silent, swift and effective communications platform will be the difference between life and death. While the ideas described previously in this manual can be an effective method of establishing a signal and response, there are better methods of conducting the disbursement of information.

Consider aligning PVC pipe in straight line configurations from one point to another. These pipes should not intersect with each other under any circumstances; they can cross over or under each other but never through a shared intersection. Place a straight-line system in between each post. This should not be that complex of a configuration, if you are keeping a low profile approach your bunker should only have between four and eight forward lookout positions. Make sure they are all tied into one another with a separate straight-line delivery system.

Use 20 oz. pop bottles as the body for the rocket. Make sure the PVC pipe is slightly larger in diameter than the body of the bottle. If the PVC pipe is too snug for the bottle to travel freely then it will get stuck and compromise the entire effectiveness of the communication system.

When a sentry at one post needs to send a message, or alert another post about a potential problem they can use the tube as part of the guidance delivery system for the rocket to ensure the message gets to the exact location without compromising the location of the intended lookout post. Keep in mind that these bottles are only going to travel a certain distance on exhausted propellant of the pressurized air variety.

To enhance performance issues associated with the post-apocalyptic PVC bottle rocket message delivery system. It is important to note that a 20-oz. pop bottle can only handle so much pressurized air before it erupts. The amount of energy released under confined conditions will cause it to travel further; it will not however send it over drastically long distances.

This is where the imagination and visualization dynamics come into play. What will pass through PVC pipe with little friction or interference? A tennis ball might be an effective and sufficient addition. It does not have to be attached to the bottle in any way, shape or form.
The message can be written in marker on the ball. Place the ball in the tube first. Pack the bottle rocket in behind it and fire away.

Of course, you will need to design a firing platform and retrieval system for clearing the PVC tube and making it ready for receiving. You can fabricate and end cap with a hole big enough to insert the bike pump nozzle. This will allow you to seal off the tube and contain the exhausted fuel source thereby promoting longer travel time. Fashion a piece of 1" thick wood to use as an end cap. Drill a hole in the center of it big enough to insert the needle for the bike pump. Make sure the needle fits snugly. Tap it into place lightly to ensure a solid seal. Leave enough of the open end of the needle exposed so that the bike pump nozzle can be secured in place. Glue the needle into place so that it will not release when the bottle rocket erupts. This end cap should remain detachable so that the spent rocket can be retrieved.

Once the rocket has been fired and the message delivered, the PVC pipe will need to be cleared of any obstructions so that a response can be received. Obviously if you leave the fired rocket in the tube delivery system any returning response will clog up in the system and a complete dismantling of that avenue will need to be conducted. Take a piece of string and tie it around the neck of the bottle. Make sure that the string is light weight yet long enough to encompass distances far greater than the rocket can ever hope to achieve. If the furthest the rocket has ever traveled is 50' in any direction, then attach 100' of string. You don't want this string to reduce the distance the rocket can achieve. Tape the opposite end of the string to the inside of the wooden end cap that has the bike needle in place.

After you hear the bottle rocket launch wait for a few seconds before removing the end cap. You can then grab the string and retrieve the bottle rocket; the tennis ball should continue to travel the length of the tube all things considered.

This idea can also be used at the defensive positions for achieving greater distance, increased accuracy and bottle rocket delivery. You can use the same principles to design a tubular launch system for your defensive bottle rocket positions. While the tripod metal rod solution will work in a pinch, a mortar type tube will increase accuracy and should provide limited additional distance.

Defensive minded survival tactics are not the only options available for hand crafted bottle rocket connoisseurs. The bunker location you have currently selected may not satisfy all our needs. Traveling to another location and getting set up to survive in a harsh non-hospitable doomsday environment will be risky to say the least. You will want to move by cover of night whenever possible and restrict day time movements to emergency situations only.

It may be impossible to travel at night over long and difficult terrain, especially since we can expect magnetic compasses to be nothing more than pocket held paper weights. Depending on the circumstances of the doomsday event, continental land mass shifting may occur, making it difficult to identify known star constellations and relate them to estimated location.

In this type of scenario, travel by night will have to be kept baring minimum distances of less than a mile. If the closest suitable survival spot happens to be a mere 50 miles away, traveling by night time caravan could take more than two months under these conditions. The added exposure to an unsafe environment is not worth the risk.

You will want to travel effectively, safely and efficiently during daylight hours without needing to worry about coming under attack. You will need to assign forward as well as flanking scout patrols. These vital assets should have a homemade bottle rocket handy. Not only can it alert others to a possible problem from a given direction, they can also be used to distract, divide and redirect possible threats from the main part of the caravan.

With proper methods and techniques in place, a flanking scout can draw the attention of the occupants of another compound or traveling party to a specific spot. This will allow the primary caravan to pass quietly from another direction with little or no significant interference. Use these devices wisely for this purpose.

A single bottle rocket being fired from a flanked position is probably not going to entice the entire adversarial unit to respond to that location, especially if they are guarding their own stock and supplies with zeal and focus. You will need to use posturing tactics to manufacture a response of the magnitude you had hoped for.

Employ a fire, forget, move and repeat method for disbursing decoy bottle rockets. This will cause confusion among the ranks at the compound as well as require a separate response. Make sure the flanking patrol continues to move in an evasive and misleading direction, stopping briefly at various points to launch another projectile.

If your traveling caravan is one that operates from an offensive minded battle plan during the doomsday aftermath, bottle rockets will come in very handy. Nothing creates panic, confusion and immediate chaos quite like incoming rounds. Granted our homemade bottle rockets are not going to be exploding shrapnel producing projectiles, but those in the besieged bunker are not going to be aware of that. A bevy of bottle rockets bouncing in from a plethora of positions outside the complex will be enough to make even the wisest warrior wobble a little bit. That little moment of insecurity may be all you need to claim victory.

Should a flammable liquid be used in place of water then these bottle rockets become better weapons of war. They will disburse a trail of vapor from launch site to landing which can be ignited to instill greater fear among the rank and file of those being attacked. Just the smell of a flammable material and the threat of lighting a fire may be all that is required to secure their surrender.

Bottle rockets alone will not be enough to mount an offensive battle plan but they can be a very effective tool when used with a little forethought and planning. Be aware that an offensive minded operation does promote the possibility of your own demise, especially in the environment of an apocalyptic aftermath, so you will want to consider your actions carefully.

Chapter 5: Stocking Supplies for Survival

Many of the materials listed above will be easy to locate should such a survivalist scenario eventually take place. Undamaged soda pop bottles are going to be another story. Most countries currently employ a recycling program for plastic products to keep pollution levels at acceptable levels. These recycling programs involve crushing and compacting of the plastic products for reuse. Once the original manufactured surface of the soda bottle has been compromised the bottle is no longer useful. Do not seek supplies of this nature for amassing useful stock. Attempting to bring the bottle back to life will be pointless. At best a bottle of this nature is going to fire into the air without any hope of accuracy.

Depending on your survival tactics you may want to begin stockpiling as many empty pop bottles as you think will be necessary. There will be plenty of them lying around either with or without contents; however, several like-minded survivalists are going to consider these objects to be a valuable commodity for several reasons. They make great storage containers for potable water storage as well as other non-perishable items of interest.

While water bottle rockets will have a purpose for the survivalist in many ways, they do not have the same effect as those produced by major fireworks manufacturers. Obtaining the raw materials needed for manufacturing destructive devices of the explosive variety requires permits to be in place prior to the doomsday event. You cannot run out to the local store and buy the supplies you would need for such devices. Even after an apocalypse finding the necessary materials and having the right tools and time to manufacture items of this nature is going to be complicated.

Clean and uncompromised pop bottles are going to be easier to find yet harder to keep and store for use as bottle rocket body parts. Depending on the quantity you have available in conjunction with how often you plan on using them, you may want to try and retrieve all previously fired rockets to reuse the bottle for another body even if you have to fabricate new fins and nose cones.

Do not attempt to substitute other plastic bottle configurations for the soda or water bottle, especially if they do not have a cylindrical shape to begin with. Using items such as plastic oil cans will be ineffective and time consuming. If you find something suitable for substitution then by all means collect it and use it accordingly. Keep in mind that although glass soda bottles have the same basic shape, they also carry more weight and therefore may not produce the same expected performance when launched.

Depending on the established site of your survival shack it might behoove you to visit a bottling or distribution facility along your travels to secure an immediate supply of pop bottles. Another option worthy of consideration would be bleach bottles of the small straight capacity sort, or plastic vegetable oil containers that may sit on shelves unused and unnoticed for several years after an apocalypse. Look for resources and substitutes wherever you can. The absence of power, utilities and commodities under these conditions will likely last years if not decades, be prepared to pass on your knowledge to those of younger age and stature.

Chapter 6: Optional Fuel Sources & Resources

As was previously mentioned there are optional fuel sources that can be used effectively with the homemade bottle rocket described in this manual. There are also optional fuel sources which can serve as a propellant when used appropriately.

Rubbing alcohol can be used in drastically reduced quantities as a propellant for achieving greater height and distance. Place a couple of drops into the plastic soda bottle, puncture a small hole in the center of the cap, secure the cap to the top of the bottle as tightly as you can, place your thumb over the hole in the cap and shake vigorously. This will vaporize the rubbing alcohol and make it extremely flammable, remove your thumb, place the rocket on the desired launching platform and place a lit ignition source near the hole in the cap. The vapors from the rubbing alcohol will ignite and expand creating pressure that will send the rocket into the sky to higher heights.

As with anything of a flammable and volatile nature you should use extreme caution and care when using techniques of this nature. If performed incorrectly this method of launching a bottle rocket can cause personal injury, property damage and in some cases fatalities.

This technique requires quick action to be effective. You cannot vaporize the alcohol, expose the hole on the cap and take several minutes to properly place the bottle rocket on the launching pad or in a mortar tube. As soon as the hole is exposed the pressurized vapor will begin to escape. If you wait too long to light the fire you are more likely to end up with an explosive bottle bomb than a working and functioning rocket.

You can also substitute the basic water bottle rocket design for aerosol cans. The contents of these objects are under intense pressure. You can duct tape a couple of wooden or metal skewers to the sides of a can in a tripod support platform, secure them into the ground at the desired launch angle and knock the spray nozzle off the can. This should send the can skyward in much the same fashion as the bottle rocket. Depending on the contents, capacity of the can as well as any other modifications you employ, this rudimentary last-minute rocket device might travel to greater heights and be more suitable for your personal survival preferences.

Anything that carries contents under pressure and has a removable escape valve can be used as a bottle rocket. You will still need to fabricate fins and mount them effectively to assist with stability and accuracy during flight, but when you are looking for something to serve a purpose anything cylindrical of this nature will suffice.

Small disposable CO_2 cartridges that are used in handgun style paintball markers might serve as an unnoticed resource for manufacturing bottle rockets. These objects are generally small in nature and come prepackaged with pressurized contents sealed within. This seal is normally punctured when the cartridge is properly connected to the fitting on the marker; however, with a little ingenuity a puncturing platform and launch retaining pad can be constructed. These can be used as small rocket propelled devices or serve as an assistive fuel source for a water bottle rocket configuration.

Regardless of which bottle rocket blueprint you elect to use as your basis for designing a homemade solution remember what rockets look like. Each of the options offered above will require further modification before being effective.

Nose cones and fins are a necessity for rockets. They are integral parts of the flight and guidance system. If you try to fire an aerosol can off without adding a nose cone and fins it is going to flop around like a fish out of water and expose everyone in the immediate area to possible injury.

Use common sense when manufacturing projectiles from common household or handy items. If it didn't work pre-apocalypse it isn't going to work in the aftermath. In other words, use vivid imagination but do not eliminate cognitive thinking in the process.

Firing a water bottle rocket using the bike pump as an air compressor involves the person operating the pump getting wet; be prepared for this event. The stream of water and air isn't going to be enough to pierce flesh but it might be enough to sting.

Whenever testing a new experimental device of this nature make sure the proper protective and safety precautions have been taken. The area in surrounding the launch pad needs to be clear of all occupants or viewers except for the person performing the pumping motion. The bike pump operator should also ensure they maintain as safe a distance as possible from the actual nose cone of the rocket as the actual timing of the launch can and will occur unexpectedly with each firing.

You should get familiar with the science and characteristics associated with rocketry as this knowledge may come in handy for making alterations. The more you know about what you are trying to do the greater chance you have of stumbling upon a successful solution.

You may not use these manmade missiles for anything other than entertainment purposes or backyard science projects but when used in conjunction with other ideas these projectiles can be extremely powerful weapons of war and survival. With the right shoulder mounted firing system and alcohol based bottle rocket propellant you can manufacture the first post-apocalyptic RPB.

Your primary career path in a post-apocalyptic planet is going to be that of an inventor. You may be reading this manual now and making mental notes of the information published within; however, when the fecal matter hits the fan you are going to forget the step by step instructions and in-depth descriptions. Not too many people even consider homemade bottle rockets as a possible inclusion in their survival plans. Either they haven't heard of it, or they have other ideas about providing safety and security for their family and followers. In most scenarios, you are going to have to think on your feet.

Depending on your reading and recollection habits the fact you are reading this material may be enough to instill the spirit and confidence in you to be able to create one of these rudimentary rockets should you eventually have the need for such an item.

Chapter 7: The Bottle Rocket Snorkel Solution

The soda pop bottle rocket device can also be used as a resource for supplying air for survivalists living in coastal regions that will be diving into fresh or salt water environments to forage for seafood.

The old bottle rockets that become dented or damaged do not necessarily have to be discarded when they are no longer serviceable for use as a projectile. 2-liter pop bottles are made from plastic. Full or empty they are buoyant. Using one of your old rockets you can make a portable floating air receptor and supplier.

Take the old bottle and either cut off the bottom of the bottle or puncture holes in all the ridges that serve as the base of the bottle. Take the top off the bottle and insert a long enough length of water tight hose. Garden hose will work; however, you may have to cut the end of the hose off to get it into the bottle. Use a water tight sealant to caulk this fitting so that the hose will not fall out or allow water to enter the bottle. The other end of the hose can be placed in the diver's mouth or attached to a water tight diving mask to be used for receiving oxygen below the waves.

It is important to note that this technique should only be used when two or more people are in the party. You will need to employ the buddy system when using this technique to ensure the safety of the swimmer. This is basically a snorkel type extension which will allow you to stay beneath the surface for longer periods of time without having to resurface to replenish air supply. The second swimmer will undertake the responsibility of making sure the floating snorkel solution remains inverted and the holes exposed to the air rather than being tugged below the sea.

Used bottle rockets can also be used as flotation devices for supporting the second swimmer. Using the basic bottle rocket concept, take a few of the older bottles, seal the cap in place, insert the nozzle of the air pump and pressurize the air in the bottle to maximum capacity, remove the pump nozzle and seal off the small hole in the bottle cap making sure it is also water tight. These devices can be placed under the arms as personal floatation equipment and keep the second swimmer relaxed and ready to respond rather than tired and ineffective due to constant treading of water. The diver might also elect to employ one of these floatation devices for rapid surfacing. Using the methods described in this paragraph, repeat the process for diver retrieval bottles. Find a large rock, stone or suitable weight and tie this to the necks of the pressurized bottles. Drop these weighted bottles to the ocean floor near where you will be diving. After the swimmer conducts their underwater excursion they can find the sunken surfacing bottles, grab the ropes, cut the cord and use the buoyancy of the bottles to help them reach the surface quicker.

This method should only be used by those familiar with working in underwater environments. There are risks involved with using any handmade substitute equipment. Prior to implementing this technique in the real world, it is highly recommended that you try it at a community pool. Use the shallow end of the pool for your experiments and perfect the technique before moving to a deeper area of the pool. Once you have mastered using the snorkel extension in a pool, transfer your knowledge to a real-world environment and take the time to practice it a couple times so that it isn't a completely new concept.

Chapter 8: Additional Areas of Interest

The soda pop bottle rocket design can be further modified by making alterations to the fins. Keep in mind this will take some ingenuity and effort to perfect the system and make it an effective and worthwhile implement; however, it may be the only possible solution for getting over an impassable object.

If you design your flight fins to incorporate hooks then the device can serve the purpose of launching a length of rope and grappling system over the edge upper edge of a cliff face or wall and with a little luck the hooks will find sufficient lodging to support the weight of a person climbing the face of the cliff.

This device might also come in handy for securing a line over a sturdy tree branch. You will need to hang hunted animals from a height that other predatory animals will not be able to reach. Being able to launch a length of rope over a branch will eliminate the need to climb the tree and risk injury to one of the members of camp.

There are several situations a survivalist might encounter where devices of this nature will be useful. Some of these situations will be evident and obvious, whereas others will become known along the way.

Of course, there are also the anti-survival scenarios for building a bottle rocket of this nature as well. Young children are often amazed at how easy it is to make a simple instrument of this nature. Helping them construct one and teaching them how to use it properly can be a very rewarding and memorable experience.

Aside from being assigned as part of a science project there are several small niche groups of bottle rocket building enthusiasts that host competitions in different locations around the country. These events can entice interested individuals to compete for design, performance, height and/or distance as well as competitive contests for rockets with and without parachutes.

These can be fun items for the family to experiment with on a hot sunny summer afternoon. Not only are they fun to watch, they spray water everywhere when they take off, which can take the edge off the heat.

They can also be an inspirational and educational tool to entice your children to use their own imagination to make alternative designs. Science possesses intricate knowledge that can be employed in many ways. We never know when one of our young children is going to see something in a different light and make the next greatest invention. Just being able to pass on significant information that they could find useful for solving an otherwise dire situation should be enough to peak your interest in spending 10 minutes to make a bottle rocket. You can never have too much information about a subject that might have important value to you in an uncertain future.

DISCLAIMER AND/OR LEGAL NOTICES: Every effort has been made to accurately represent this book and it's potential. Results vary with every individual, and your results may or may not be different from those depicted. No promises, guarantees or warranties, whether stated or implied, have been made that you will produce any specific result from this book. Your efforts are individual and unique, and may vary from those shown. Your success depends on your efforts, background and motivation.

The material in this publication is provided for educational and informational purposes only and is not intended as medical advice. The information contained in this book should not be used to diagnose or treat any illness, metabolic disorder, disease or health problem. Always consult your physician or health care provider before beginning any nutrition or exercise program. Use of the programs, advice, and information contained in this book is at the sole choice and risk of the reader.